PENNSYLVANIA

LET'S EXPLORE AMERICA

PENNSYLVANIA
Valerie Bodden

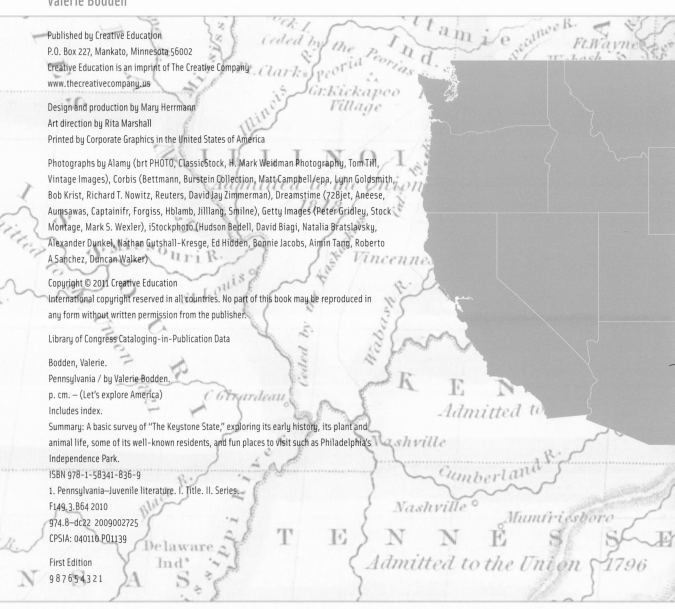

Published by Creative Education
P.O. Box 227, Mankato, Minnesota 56002
Creative Education is an imprint of The Creative Company
www.thecreativecompany.us

Design and production by Mary Herrmann
Art direction by Rita Marshall
Printed by Corporate Graphics in the United States of America

Photographs by Alamy (brt PHOTO, ClassicStock, H. Mark Weidman Photography, Tom Till, Vintage Images), Corbis (Bettmann, Burstein Collection, Matt Campbell/epa, Lynn Goldsmith, Bob Krist, Richard T. Nowitz, Reuters, David Jay Zimmerman), Dreamstime (728jet, Aneese, Aumsawas, Captainifr, Forgiss, Hblamb, Jilllang, Smilne), Getty Images (Peter Gridley, Stock Montage, Mark S. Wexler), iStockphoto (Hudson Bedell, David Biagi, Natalia Bratslavsky, Alexander Dunkel, Nathan Gutshall-Kresge, Ed Hidden, Bonnie Jacobs, Aimin Tang, Roberto A Sanchez, Duncan Walker)

Library of Congress Cataloging-in-Publication Data

Bodden, Valerie.
Pennsylvania / by Valerie Bodden.
p. cm. – (Let's explore America)
Includes index.
Summary: A basic survey of "The Keystone State," exploring its early history, its plant and animal life, some of its well-known residents, and fun places to visit such as Philadelphia's Independence Park.
ISBN 978-1-58341-836-9
1. Pennsylvania–Juvenile literature. I. Title. II. Series.
F149.3.B64 2010
974.8–dc22   2009002725
CPSIA: 040110 P01139

First Edition
9 8 7 6 5 4 3 2 1

C CREATIVE EDUCATION

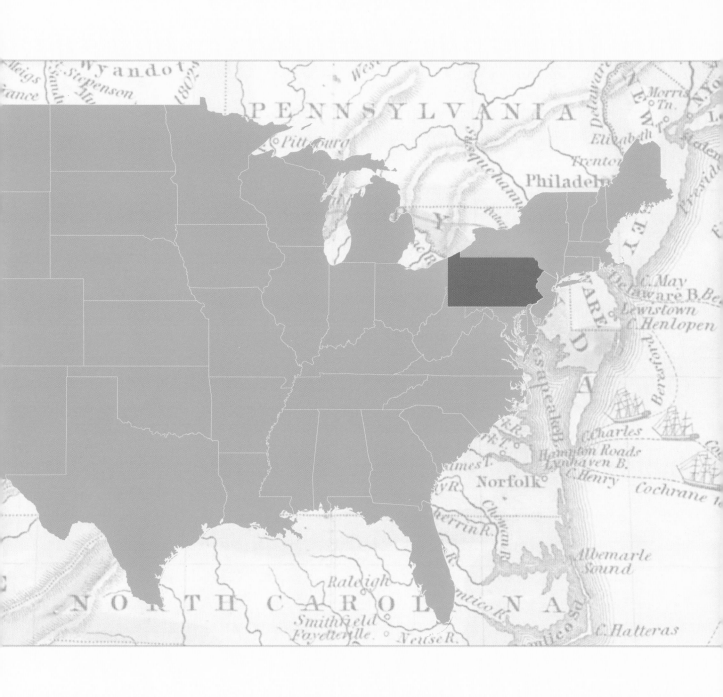

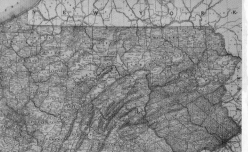

TOP, THEN LEFT TO RIGHT:

- *William Penn (the man Pennsylvania was named after) buying land from Indians*
- *An old map of Pennsylvania*
- *Horses at a Pennsylvania farm*
- *The United States' Constitution, which was signed in Pennsylvania*
- *William Penn*

Pennsylvania is a state in the eastern part of America. It is a medium-sized state. Pennsylvania became a state in 1787. Pennsylvania is nicknamed "The **Keystone** State." This is because it helped keep the states together when America became a country.

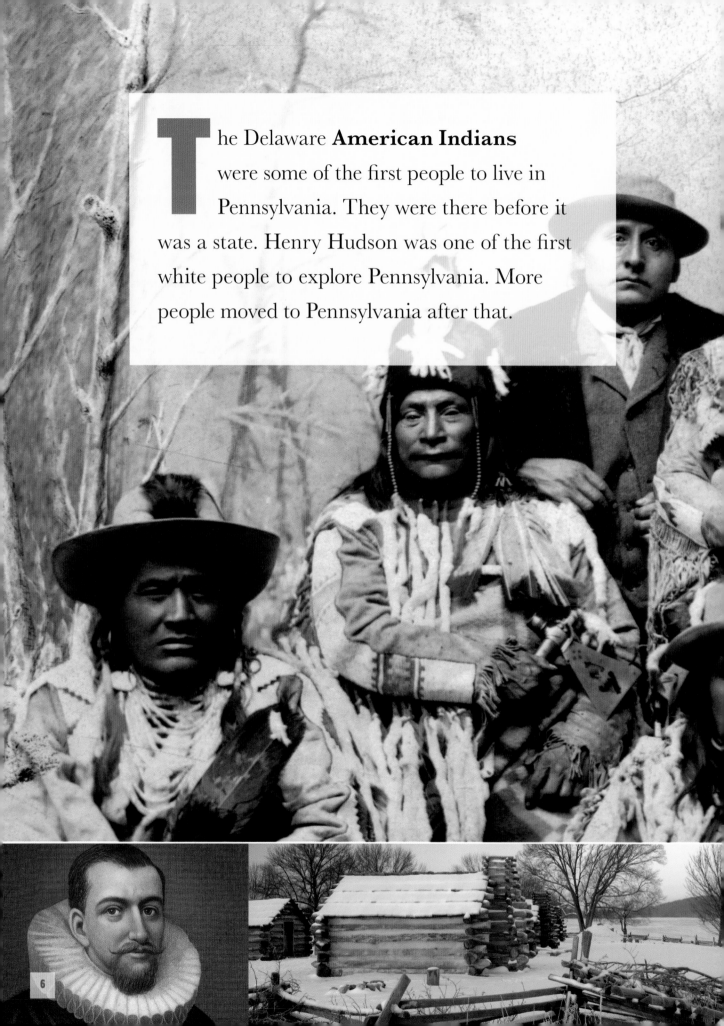

The Delaware **American Indians** were some of the first people to live in Pennsylvania. They were there before it was a state. Henry Hudson was one of the first white people to explore Pennsylvania. More people moved to Pennsylvania after that.

TOP, THEN LEFT TO RIGHT:
- *American Indians of Pennsylvania*
- *Explorer Henry Hudson*
- *Old log cabins in Pennsylvania*
- *Houses in Philadelphia, Pennsylvania, from the 1700s*
- *Workers in a Pennsylvania steel factory*

TOP, THEN LEFT TO RIGHT:

- *The Delaware River in Pennsylvania*
- *A Pennsylvania lake*
- *A snowy Pennsylvania field in the winter*
- *A covered bridge*

Pennsylvania is covered with lots of **mountains** and hills. Many rivers and streams flow through Pennsylvania. There are lots of lakes, too. Summers in Pennsylvania are warm and rainy. Winters are cold and snowy.

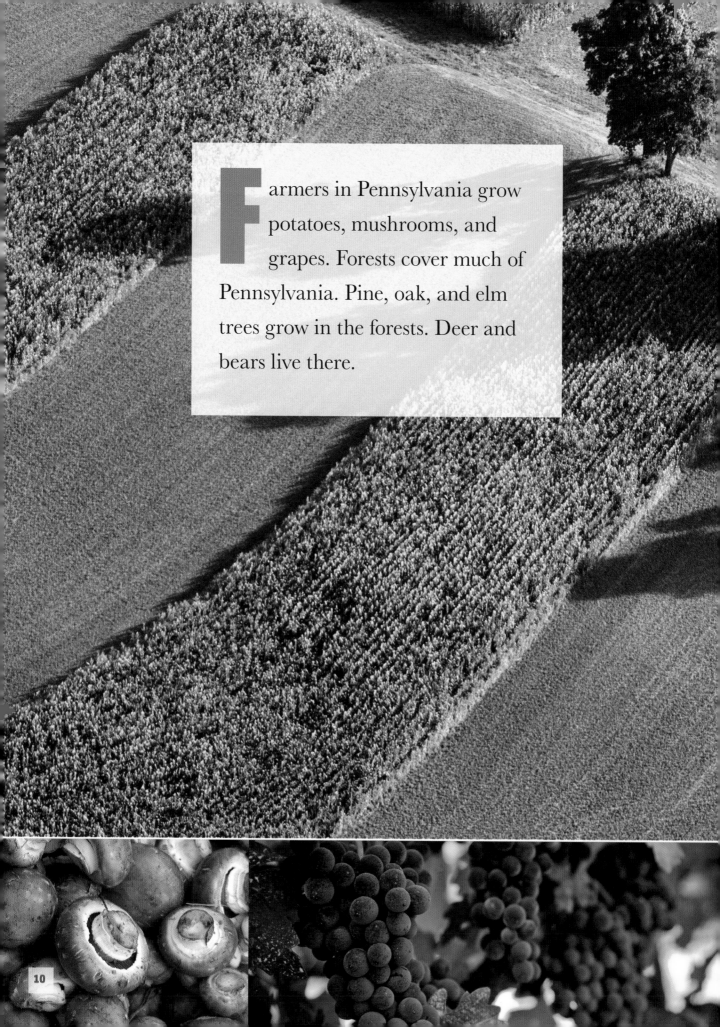

Farmers in Pennsylvania grow potatoes, mushrooms, and grapes. Forests cover much of Pennsylvania. Pine, oak, and elm trees grow in the forests. Deer and bears live there.

TOP, THEN LEFT TO RIGHT:
- *Pennsylvania farm fields*
- *Mushrooms*
- *Grapes*
- *A deer in a Pennsylvania forest*
- *Potatoes*

Pennsylvania's state flower is the mountain laurel. The mountain laurel is a bush with pink or white flowers. Pennsylvania's state bird is the ruffed grouse. The ruffed grouse is a brown, black, and white bird. Pennsylvania's state tree is the eastern hemlock. The eastern hemlock is an **evergreen** tree.

TOP, THEN LEFT TO RIGHT:
- *A forest of eastern hemlock trees*
- *A ruffed grouse*
- *Mountain laurels*
- *Hemlock tree branches*

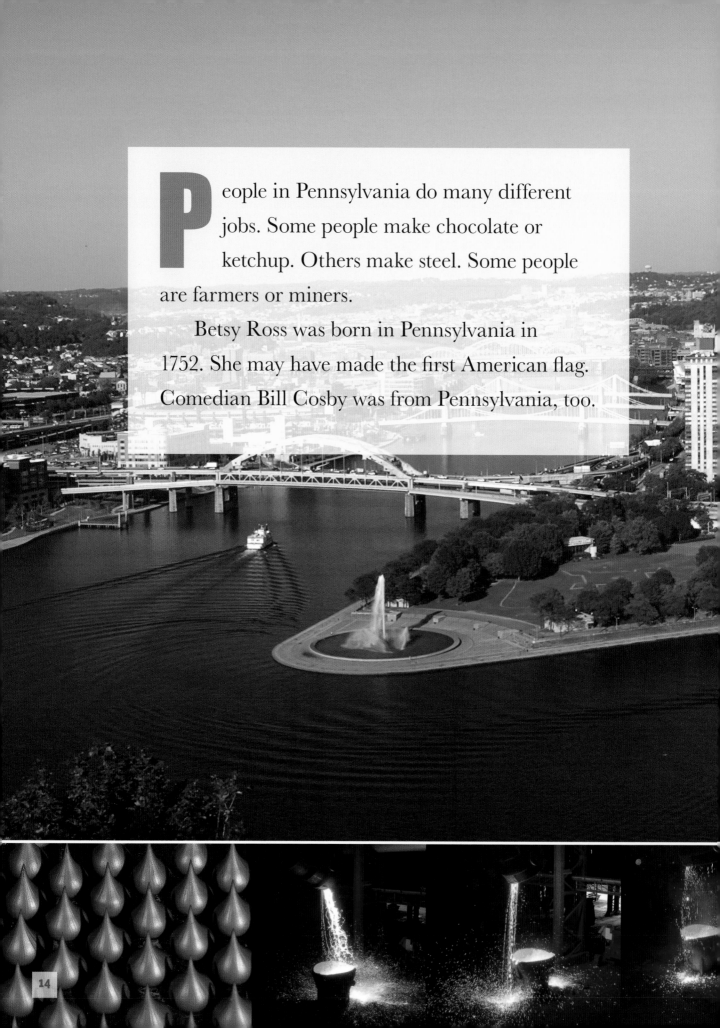

People in Pennsylvania do many different jobs. Some people make chocolate or ketchup. Others make steel. Some people are farmers or miners.

Betsy Ross was born in Pennsylvania in 1752. She may have made the first American flag. Comedian Bill Cosby was from Pennsylvania, too.

TOP, THEN LEFT TO RIGHT:

- *Rivers around downtown Pittsburgh, Pennsylvania*
- *Hershey's chocolate candies*
- *A steel mill in Pittsburgh*
- *Comedian Bill Cosby*
- *Betsy Ross sewing a flag*

Philadelphia is the biggest city in Pennsylvania. Almost 1.5 million people live there. Harrisburg is the capital of Pennsylvania. The capital is where people in the **government** make decisions about laws for the state.

TOP, THEN LEFT TO RIGHT:
- *The city of Philadelphia at night*
- *People and traffic on the streets of Harrisburg*
- *The state capitol (main government building) in Harrisburg*
- *The round ceiling of the capitol*
- *Books about state laws*

17

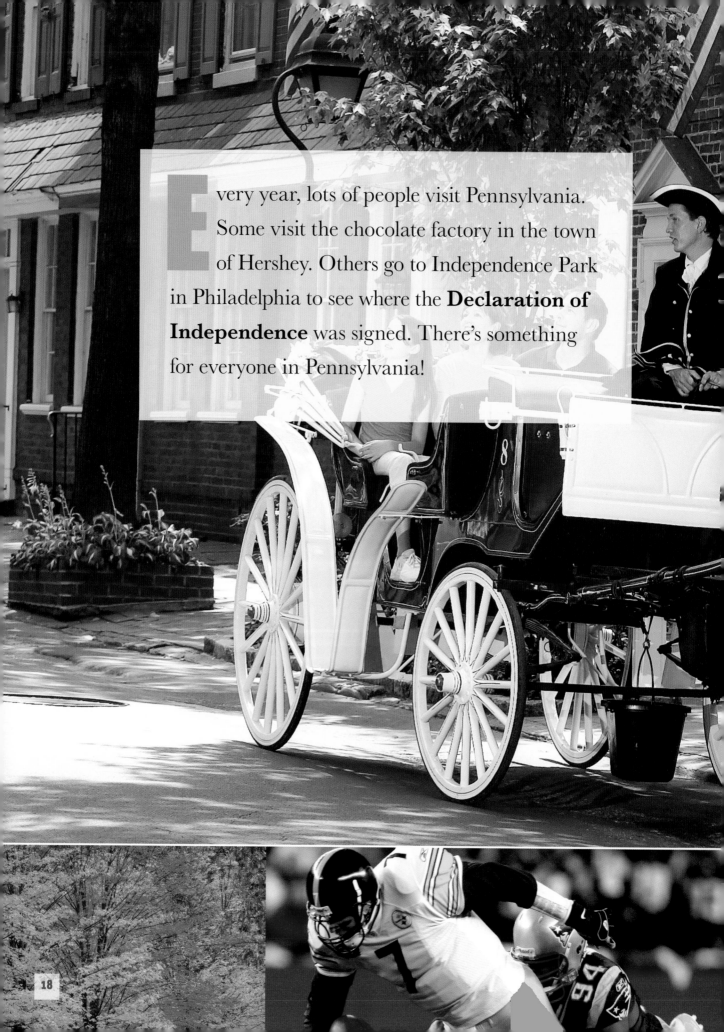

Every year, lots of people visit Pennsylvania. Some visit the chocolate factory in the town of Hershey. Others go to Independence Park in Philadelphia to see where the **Declaration of Independence** was signed. There's something for everyone in Pennsylvania!

TOP, THEN LEFT TO RIGHT:
- A horse and old-fashioned wagon in Philadelphia
- Pennsylvania trees in the fall
- A Pittsburgh Steelers football player
- Punxsutawney Phil, a famous groundhog in Pennsylvania
- People acting out important battles of the past in Pennsylvania

19

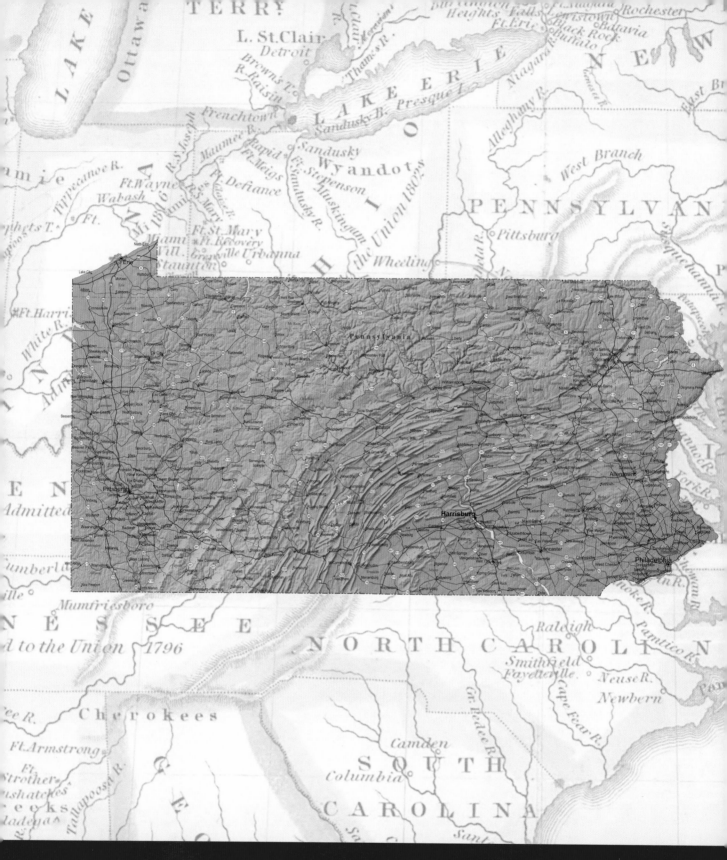

FACTS ABOUT PENNSYLVANIA

First year as a state: *1787*

Population: *12,604,767*

Capital: *Harrisburg*

Biggest city: *Philadelphia*

Nickname: *The Keystone State*

State bird: *ruffed grouse*

State flower: *mountain laurel*

State tree: *eastern hemlock*

Pennsylvania cherry trees in the spring

GLOSSARY

American Indians—people who lived in America before white people arrived

Declaration of Independence—the written statement that made America its own country

evergreen—a plant that keeps its leaves or needles all year long

government—a group that makes laws for the people of a state or country

keystone—the middle stone in an arch that holds the other stones in place, or something that holds the pieces around it together

mountains—very tall, steep hills made out of rock

READ MORE

Heinrichs, Ann. *Pennsylvania*. New York: Children's Press, 2006.

Kane, Kristen. *K Is for Keystone: A Pennsylvania Alphabet*. Chelsea, Mich.: Sleeping Bear Press, 2003.

LEARN MORE

Enchanted Learning: Pennsylvania
http://www.enchantedlearning.com/usa/states/pennsylvania/index.shtml
This site has Pennsylvania facts, maps, and coloring pages.

Kids Konnect: Pennsylvania
http://www.kidskonnect.com/content/view/202/27
This site lists facts about Pennsylvania.

A Pennsylvania farmer plowing a
field the old-fashioned way

A frozen Pennsylvania lake in the winter